# Ned
# KELLY

WHO WAS...

# Ned
# KELLY

## Gangster hero of
## the Australian Outback

## CHARLIE BOXER

✳ SHORT BOOKS

Published in 2004 by
Short Books
15 Highbury Terrace
London N5 1UP

10 9 8 7 6 5 4 3 2

A CIP catalogue record for this book
is available from the British Library.

ISBN 1-904095-61-5

Printed in Great Britain by
Bookmarque, Croydon, Surrey.

# The Drop

As he was led into the execution chamber, Ned tried to picture the crowd waiting in the sunshine outside – a huge crowd, according to the priest who had given him the last rites. Since his conviction, there had been petitions, marches and demonstrations to save his life. And now a dejected mob, some five thousand of Australia's rootless poor, had gathered in a ring of silent protest around the prison walls.

But Ned knew he would not be saved now. The beam from which he was going to swing was grooved and notched with the marks left by the hundreds of men hanged before him. Ned's eyes flashed around the room, and came to rest on a policeman standing guard at the posts below – so close he could smell the starch on that hateful uniform.

For an instant the policeman returned his gaze, with equal disdain. As far as he was concerned, Ned Kelly was the opposite of a hero, nothing more than a filthy, low-down police killer who'd made a fool of the authorities and rubbished the good name of his country around the world. Hanging was too good for him. Yet he had to concede something to this man: here he was, moments from a horrible, spine-wrenching death, and still he seemed ripe for a fight.

The noose was put over Ned's head, and pulled tight; blood pulsed through his veins. But he never took his eyes off that policeman. He would show those lily-livered British officers how to die. For he was Ned Kelly, the last of the bushrangers, the most spectacular rebel ever to have stood up to all those splay-footed, wombat-headed bastards – the policemen, the judges and the ranch-owners who ran Australia, the foulest hole on earth.

He was Ned Kelly, son of Red – and wasn't Red

the finest Irishman ever to have suffered at the hands of those blue-coated officers of the English crown? And hadn't Ned vowed, the day he'd buried his dad, that he would take revenge?

As St Patrick had rid Ireland of its snakes, he would cleanse Australia of its policemen. In a coat of armour too black and coarse to reflect a glint of the vivid Australian moon, he would haunt the bush like a vengeful saint and make the country pure again...

And so, filled with dreams, Ned lurched to his doom.

# The Gold Rush

It was only a hundred years before Ned Kelly was hanged in Melbourne in the spring of 1880 that the first prison ships had sailed out from the British Isles. The convicts had arrived in their thousands to find a sterile and waterless land – one vast prison from which escape was impossible. Chained in long, winding lines, they were set to work, ruled over by masters who carried whips and mumbled the Lord's Prayer morning, noon and execution time.

Those convicts who survived the disease, the starvation and the merciless flogging dreamed obsessively of revenge. Their spirits yearned for a saviour who would rise up and destroy their masters. So terrible were the early days that this lust for vengeance remained the dominant religion of Australian life for a long time after the last convict regained his freedom.

Red Kelly, Ned's father, was one of those last convicts – shipped out to Australia at the age of 18. With his own country, Ireland, on the brink of famine, he had stolen a pig to feed his starving brothers and sisters. Sentenced to seven years' hard labour, he had been despatched to the other side of the world.

Ned's mother's family, on the other hand, had left Ireland of their own free will. Ellen Quinn, Ned's mother, was just nine years old when her parents had decided to emigrate and make a fresh start. The Quinns sailed for Australia in the same year Red was transported, landing as free settlers in the colony of Victoria – all ten of them, mother, father and eight children. They bought a small farm, where they tended a few cows and pigs, as they had done back home.

Around the time of Ellen's 18th birthday, Red had regained his freedom, and was travelling around

Victoria looking for somewhere to settle down. Ellen, who had never left her parents' farm in nine years, had grown into a luminous, dark-haired beauty. She remembered all her life the day the big, strong Irishman, with flaming red hair, walked through the farmhouse door.

There is no record of Red and Ellen's romance, except that Ellen's parents must have disapproved, for the pair eloped several hundred miles to Melbourne to be married. On their return home, the couple made their peace with the family; Red started working on the farm, and Ellen's first child, a daughter was born (she died in infancy). But it was not long before the young Kellys were on the move again.

A few years previously, over in America, a nugget of gold had been found on the bed of a little Californian creek. The Gold Rush of 1849 drew hundreds of thousands of people to America from all corners of the earth. Among them were many Australians, one of whom noticed that he was panning gold from a terrain very like the bush around his home in Victoria. He sold his stake, and hurried back to Australia where he struck lucky all over again. Thus began the great Australian Gold Rush.

Once you knew how to look for it, gold could be found in small amounts all over the young country. And, after the birth of Ellen's second child, another daughter, Red joined the rush, digging his hole in the swarming gold-fields of Bendigo, in Northern Victoria. Like most diggers, Red never struck it rich, but he managed to pull just enough out of the ground to buy a small farm of his own where he and Ellen could live and bring up a family. They moved in just before Ned was born.

The farm was outside Beveridge, a town of just one short street and a pub, but Red reckoned that with all the gold traffic running along the road, Beveridge would swell out like other gold-rush towns had done, and bring prosperity and security to all its inhabitants. There was much to be improved on the new property, which had remained long untended, but Red set to work with high hopes – he bought wood for making fences, and building materials and a new set of tools.

Just as suddenly as the tide of gold had arrived, however, it seemed to ebb away again, luring the diggers after it and leaving hundreds of small farmers like Red Kelly stranded with debt and bad investments.

He also faced another problem. Before the flush of his optimism had run dry, he had written to his family back home, persuading them that a better life awaited them in Australia than they would ever know in Ireland. And now, just as the bad times were descending on the Kelly homestead, a boat-load of his brothers and sisters arrived.

The Kelly clan may have come with the best of intentions, but they did not bring Red and Ellen the support they hoped for; rather, they initiated their descent into infamy. It was from this time that Red started to get into trouble with the law once more.

Unable to find work, he and his brothers turned to horse and cattle thieving to make a living. They made a bad name for themselves: the authorities pursued them, their more law-abiding neighbours avoided them. The debts piled up, and eventually the farm outside Beveridge had to be sold.

Red and Ellen, with five children to care for, now found themselves almost continuously on the move. From one broken-down farmstead to another they went, always trailing a wake of disapproval and suspicion behind them.

# The Little Man

From the day he was born, Ned stood out as his father's great hope for the future. As a baby he was plucky and cheerful, as a boy he was strong and burly and displayed a fine, defiant temper.

By the time he was 11 years old, he was as powerful as a man, and would fight all comers in defence of his family name. He was the last piece of unalloyed good fortune that old Red Kelly knew.

Ned felt his parents' frustrations keenly, and he blamed the rich landowners for their troubles.

'Why does it bother them, Dad, if you take a cow

now and then?' he asked. 'Haven't they got enough already?'

Red had no answers except to feed his son's anger. 'It's because we're Irish, Ned,' he would reply. 'That's why they hate us so.'

Of all the many ex-convict families that stayed in early Australia – English, Irish, Scottish, Welsh – it was the Irish, in particular, who had the greatest trouble throwing off their clouded past and who were most likely to remain outcast in the young country.

Among these families, resentment of British authority was bitterer than it had ever been in Ireland and many of them got so used to living with perpetual misfortune that their will collapsed.

Ned, though, was different. Decisive and re-sourceful, he was one of those boys who want to be the cause of everything that happens to them, who insist on dealing the cards that decide their own fate. He grew up fast. The soft, pale skin of his boyhood roughened up, his large brown eyes narrowed and his lips turned inward and thin, and yet his face kept its cheerful good spirits, and his swarm of uncles and aunts and grandparents still grabbed the little man on to their laps, whenever he walked by.

*\*\**

After they left Beveridge, Red took his family to live outside the little village of Avenel, a prosperous enclave with a village green and big houses set in grounds modelled on English ducal parks. The villagers did not extend a warm welcome to the Kellys, who, with their furtive eyes and worn clothes, already had the look of trouble about them.

Australia in those days was still in many ways a troubled place. The ex-convict families not only resented the police, as the face of authority in the country; they also resented the rich, and in particular the rich landowners – a legacy of the way that the land had been shared out in the colony right at the start.

Years back, when this part of Australia was off-limits to everyone, wealthy cattle-ranchers had explored and surveyed the virgin territory south west of New South Wales, and illegally seized all the best bits. The poor settlers had arrived to find only the worst scraps left for them, from which they had to try and scrape their living, while beside them huge ranches were already established, with herds of cattle and flocks of sheep tended by strings of fine horses.

The Kellys knew all too well that the land that was on offer to them near Avenel was a rotten patch, but it was all they could afford. They also knew they would get no help from their smart neighbours, who already had them marked down as a bunch of losers.

The villagers had not reckoned on the spirit of young Ned, though.

One blazing afternoon, Ned was wandering through the empty bush, when he caught sight of the son of one of the rich landowners walking about a quarter of a mile away.

Both boys knew that their fathers hated each other; and, as they slowly, inevitably drew together, like two specks of dust in an empty region of space, each affected nonchalance.

The well-dressed boy looked at the sky, he looked at the ground, he looked at a flock of cocka-toos swarming through the air, and then, while indolently eyeing the swirling waters of a flooded creek, he tripped and stumbled in. He was not a strong swimmer, and soon he began to drown.

Ned ran over, immediately dived in. He swam to the flailing boy and dragged him to the bank. He tugged him up the slippery sides, and shook him till all the water spluttered out. When at last the boy opened his eyes, he looked confusedly into his saviour's face.

'That's what comes of being such a bloody fairy!' Ned laughed at him.

Ned's rescue of Dick Shelton made a big splash in the news-starved district. All the respectable folk of Avenel agreed it was a good sign that a Kelly child had been so public-spirited as to risk his life to save Dick. They got together and presented him with a prize: a fine green sash, embroidered and fringed with brocade of gold.

The gold on the deep emerald green was an acknowledgement of Ned's Irishness, and a recognition that he had earned the reputation of being a brave, Irish lad. This green sash became Ned's banner of Irish pride, and he carried it with him through all his short life's tribulations.

# The Death of Red

Ned's rescue of the Shelton boy did not change things in Avenel for long. The local ranch-owners, for all that they admired young Ned, strongly disapproved of the shifty Kelly clan. Horses and cattle were going missing, and they nagged the police to keep the family under watch.

One day, when Ned was ten, a Welsh farmer called Morgan burst into the Kelly hut, a posse of policemen flocked in behind him like a swarm of mangy crows.

'Red Kelly,' Morgan spluttered, 'I told you what I'd do if you stole a cow again!'

The policemen started to poke carelessly about the hut. In their clumsy search, much was broken, and the few provisions they found were tipped on to the floor and spoiled. Morgan positioned himself like a judge over a rank-smelling barrel which stood in a corner of the room, and put his hand inside. Through a cloud of flies he pulled out a piece of maggoty beef:

'What have we here then?' he asked, with pointed sarcasm.

Meanwhile, in the ash-heap beside the hut a policeman had found a half-burnt cowhide with its brand cut out. Red Kelly was taken into custody, and the next week was sentenced to six months' hard labour. His last words before he was taken away were to Ned: 'Look after your mother and the little ones.'

As Ned lay in bed and heard his mother crying through the night he swore to himself he would protect her and provide for his brothers and sisters. He swore that one day he would punish those policemen and make them sorry for every one of his mother's tears. One day...

The trials of prison life hit Red Kelly hard, and he

came out a broken man. For three days he went on a drinking binge, and then arrived home drunk. Within a year he died, bloated as a beached whale.

The sadness of his young death bored a hole in Ned's heart. Years later he would try to remind the world of his vanished father by declaring he was 'Ned Kelly, son of Red Kelly, and a finer man never stood in two shoes'. He clung on to everything his father had ever taught him – Red showing him how to pan for gold in the creek behind the hut; how to approach an untethered horse in the dark and slip up on its back; and how to hide your tracks through the midnight bush.

Ned vowed to make himself into a successful incarnation of all his father's failures.

\*\*\*

Ned's first duty as head of the family was to report his father's death to the town police. He had to walk the three miles to the station barefoot. Two officers looked up, recognised him, and returned to their conversation, ignoring his tear-stained face.

'My father, Red Kelly, died yesterday,' announced

Ned. One of the policemen sat up at this, looking genuinely sympathetic.

'Sorry to hear that kid,' he said, and put a hand out to pat the boy's shoulder.

But Ned wouldn't look at him. After a long silence, the same policeman spoke again, 'We'll have to make a report on that.'

Ned stayed staring at the floor but he sensed the two policemen glance at each other with suppressed satisfaction as they wrote up the details of their old enemy's death. Nothing was said out loud, but Ned felt the barbs of a thousand provocations. He signed his name in the big book, 'Edward Kelly', and gave his shaky, childish signature just the same brave flourish his father had always affected.

# Harry Power

A money-less widow with seven children in 19th-century Australia was bound to have a struggle to hold her family together. Twice Ellen was given a lecture by the local magistrate about using abusive language and threatening behaviour. The children, too, were beginning to get into trouble. It was time for a change, and one evening she announced, 'We're leaving Avenel and going to stay with your aunts in Greta.'

Greta was a small hamlet 50 miles up-country, a two-day journey along the old wagoners' route. Ellen's two sisters were both grass-widows, which meant that their husbands were in jail, also for cattle stealing. So Ellen and her sisters had decided to lump their misfortunes together, and bring up all of their 17 children on one hilly back-country farm.

Their Quinn cousins welcomed Ellen and her children warmly at Greta. Soon the kids were chasing each other around the gum trees and exploring the scrubby hills nearby. Ned's cousins showed him caves and pits, where you could hide ten cows easily and no one could find them, and trees from whose branches you could see every track in the valley, great for keeping a look-out for anyone on your trail.

It was a squash in the slab hut, but other grandparents and more cousins lived nearby. There was endless coming and going, and every now and then some kids would be sent off to stay somewhere else. Ned always remembered to look after his mother and siblings, but there was little he could do to defend his family against the mysterious self-destructiveness of the adults around him.

One night he woke to hear noises at the door. His uncle, Jim Kelly, was outside. Ned shook his mother. 'Uncle Jimmy's here Mum.'

Though she was fast asleep, Ellen's immediate reaction was one of hostility and alarm. 'Don't let him in!'

Jimmy had already entered, however, and was feeling around in the dark for his sister-in-law: 'Ellen? Where are you?'

Ellen whispered fiercely across the room, 'Get out you drunk bastard.' As he moved towards her voice, Jimmy tripped over a body sleeping on the floor. A baby started crying. Jimmy paused for a while, and then in the dark Ned and Ellen heard a bottle being uncorked, and a rough old mouth taking a long noisy slug of drink.

Ellen wasn't going to have any more of this, and she began to push Jim Kelly backwards towards the door. He wrapped his arms around her and whispered something in her ear. Ellen shoved the slob outside and smashed his bottle of gin over his head before barring the door.

'Go to sleep Ned,' she said, as she crawled back under her blanket.

However, half-an-hour later Uncle Jimmy staggered back from somewhere with a flaming brand and set it to the shack. The first whiff of smoke and

Ellen guessed what Jimmy was up to. She got everyone out of a back window. The dry, bark walls of the hut blazed up as suddenly as if they had been dipped in pitch. The noise of the fire woke everyone in the township of Greta, and a crowd rushed towards the hut knowing that if anyone needed saving, it was already too late. No one carried anything from the blaze, except young Ned, who stood in the night clinging to his green sash.

\*\*\*

Ellen now decided to move her children away one more time and set up on her own. She looked at a number of cheap properties and chose an 80-acre plot not far from Greta on a boggy little river called Eleven Mile Creek.

The hut was even more primitive than their previous homes, built of slabs of bark leaning together like a card house. But there were definite advantages; the soil wasn't too bad, the rent was low, there were no neighbours to row with and no mobs of attractive horses roaming loose in pastures nearby. The farm stood quite by itself between the creek and the road. Ellen could supplement her income by providing a bit of food, shelter, and a sly glass of grog to the few travellers who passed by.

Ned, though barely 13, already had an adult head on his shoulders. This little farm, he realised, presented him and his brothers and sisters with their first, and last, opportunity to escape a life of trouble. If they could just get the farm going and raise decent crops, then they might buck the family pattern of small-scale pilfering, a pattern which inevitably escalated into a running battle with the police and neighbouring farmers.

First, the ground had to be cleared. Virgin bush spawned trees of an incredible obduracy, whose trunks could shatter an iron axe. Every stump had to be burnt out, and every rock and spiny root had to be prized from the ground and carted away. To clear ten acres could take a family a whole winter. And only when the land was completely cleared could ploughing begin. But this was the hardest job of all: in places, the virgin soil had been so compacted over dry millennia that it was harder than concrete and would crumble any but the most expensive modern plough.

Still, they made a go of it. And a daily routine of sorts set in – Ellen making a bit of money after the working day, by dispensing grog and chat to migrant workers travelling down the road.

One day, as the sun was going down, a stranger approached the hut. He walked right up to the door before asking, 'Is this Ellen Kelly's place?' The stranger was past the best years of his life – what had once been a bushy orange beard had grown a little peppery, and his high whiskery voice chuckled and wheezed. But, though he was dusty and tired, his eyes shone like an old-time gold prospector returning to his strike

'Come in and sit down,' said Ned, 'I'll call Mum.'

'You must be Ned?' he winked. Ned nodded and ran to fetch his mother.

From the threshold of her hut, Ellen Kelly greeted the stranger with a blunt, 'Yes?'

The man looked at her, blinking, and explained that one of her brothers-in-law had told him to come here – 'Tom Lloyd, your sister's husband?'

'And where do you know him from?' Ellen asked.

'Pentridge Jail.'

'How's he doing?' Ellen asked.

'Oh, he's getting along.'

'When did you last see him?'

'About three days ago,' the man replied. And, as Ellen looked him up and down, she began to appreciate that this was no ordinary wayfarer.

'How d'you come to leave Pentridge?' she asked.

'Over the wall,' he said, and chuckled. No one had escaped from Pentridge for a long time, but Ellen didn't doubt his story for a moment. 'So what's your name?' she asked.

'Harry Power,' he replied. 'Tom said you had a good, lonely place, and you wouldn't mind letting me lie low for a few days.'

Harry Power was a well-known bushranger. The bushrangers – outlaws and highwaymen – were Australia's Robin Hoods, known to share with the poor what they stole from the rich. They were as famous as film stars and as glamorous as Jesse James, but they were a dying breed; hunted to extinction by a police force equipped with the technology of the new age, especially the telegraph and the railway. To have a bushranger turn up at your hut like this was the dream of every lonely Australian boy and girl stuck in the monotony of the outback.

Ellen gave Harry everything he needed. And, after a few days he moved on. But every month or so he dropped by Ellen's hut, on his way somewhere or other. He clearly had a shine for Ned and one afternoon he rode up and asked the boy straight out, 'Fancy coming for a ride with me?'

So Ned accompanied Harry on his first raid. They stole a horse from a nearby ranch, and took it on a long trip into the bush, where they met someone who bought it from Harry. Ned began to spend days and nights in the bush with the old man; they rode the trackless waste, stealing horses and sticking up rich travellers. Posters with Harry's picture on them appeared throughout the country. The posters said that he was accompanied by a tall, dark lad. Everyone had their suspicions as to who this lad was, but no one ever got close enough to swear it was Ned Kelly.

Old Harry Power loved the life of the bushranger, and liked to behave as if he was the last of them. He blazed a flagrant trail, always letting his victims know who had robbed them, and beamed with pleasure when he saw his name and face on a 'WANTED' poster.

He jeered at the police, boasting he would never be caught – and certainly not in his hide-out in the bush, for the peacock that guarded him there was more vigilant and reliable than a pack of Irish mastiffs.

But Harry's friends all knew where this hideout was, and some two years later, for what reasons no one knows, one of Ellen's brothers suddenly betrayed its location to the police.

The police surprised the sleeping bush-ranger one drizzly morning. The famous peacock, as vain as Harry Power himself, was keeping its feathers dry out of the rain and never crowed once.

# The Fight

Ned, 15 now, appeared in court at Harry's trial, but there was neither evidence nor positive identification to convict him. The police, however, remained convinced that he was Harry Power's apprentice, and marked him down as a lad who needed the flashness taken out of him.

They got their first chance to take him down a rung a few weeks after Harry was sent to jail, when a travelling hawker passing through the country with his wagon of pots and pans complained to the police about the teenager. There had been a disagreement over a roaming horse, which had descended into a fight, and then Ned had sent the hawker's wife a parcel of calves' balls. When the hawker realised how hard the police intended to hammer the boy he withdrew his complaint, but the police proceeded regardless, and Ned was given three months in Beechworth town jail for disturbing the peace.

In his short life, Ned had already notched up a fair amount of experience of the criminal life. Two years as Harry Power's apprentice had taught him plenty. Now, though, as he embarked on his first stint behind bars, he developed the hard pride of a boy who relishes every confrontation with the law. He got on famously with the jail's inmates and savoured their stories, which always seemed to end with a policeman lying in the dust.

Back at home after his sentence was over, Ned took to sitting around and chatting with the characters that came to his mother's hut for grog. He made fast friends with one in particular – 'Wild' Wright – a notorious fairground-fighter, whose trademark was to barge his way to the front of a crowded bar on a Saturday night, booming out, 'Men first, dogs last!'

One evening Wright found that his horse had

strayed. 'Lend me yours Ned, and you can have mine when she shows up.'

This was a kind of present in Ned's mind, for Wright's horse was a beautiful roan mare, and when Ned found her the next day he got straight up on her back and rode into Wangaratta, the nearest big town.

He let a few girls he liked ride her, and for two days he lived it up in town, parading the magnificent animal up and down the streets. But out of the police-station window he was being watched – Constable Edward Hall, a 16-stone giant, reckoned the horse must be stolen.

'Hey, Ned Kelly!' Hall called out from the porch, 'Come here, mate. There's some papers for you to sign regarding your release.'

Ned had actually been friends with Hall once and so he rode over. As he dismounted the policeman seized him, and Ned understood he was about to be locked up again. With mad teenage fury he cracked open the giant's bear-hug and scrambled for the horse.

'Don't!' said Hall, and pulled his revolver on Ned.

'Don't you!' said Ned, but Hall squeezed the trigger. The gun didn't fire. Damned if a teenager would escape him, Hall tried again to pull the trigger, and again the bullet failed to strike.

Hall now pointed his gun one more time and Ned threw himself on top of the policeman, knocking him into the dust. Unable to prize the gun from his monstrous hand, Ned slipped his legs round his girth and dug his spurs into his blue-coated back making the policeman roar like a calf attacked by dogs.

Two more policemen now trundled out of the station and joined in the fight. Ned boasted afterwards that he was chucking the three of them about 'like dung around a paddock' and that he was only subdued when the local blacksmith joined the crush.

Wright's horse did indeed turn out to have been stolen, and a few days later Ned was charged with horse-stealing and sentenced to three years' hard labour. Poor Ned, he had transgressed into a world where grudges were passed around from rich farmers to policemen to magistrates as freely as cakes are handed round at a party. It was pretty bitter to be sent down for so long when everyone accepted that you had not known that you were doing anything wrong.

In prison, the warders took an instant dislike to the cocky teenager with his insolent grin and tried to break him. He served his sentence either cracking rocks on a chain gang, or locked up in solitary.

Ned was 19 years old when he next went home. He swore to his mother, he'd rather face the gallows than go back to jail again. But he knew he could not hang around the farm for long: the police would surely trip him up again. He set off to a job in a sawmill some distance away, and for a year he worked his way around Australia, and didn't get into trouble once. Nor did he earn any reputation except that of being a solid bloke and an unbeatable fist fighter.

Once, he met up again with Wild Wright, 'You bastard,' he said, 'why didn't you tell me the bloody horse was stolen?' They fought 20 rounds, after which Wright testified he had never met anyone as tough or as strong as young Ned Kelly.

## 'I never shot a man yet!'

While he was on his travels, bad news began to reach Ned about what was going on at home. People who had passed through Wangaratta told of how his 16-year-old brother, Dan, had been up before the court and that the first jail terms were being handed down to the rising generation. Though it would expose him to danger, Ned decided he must go back and try to steer Dan from further trouble.

The home he returned to was happier than he had ever known it before. Ellen had recently re-married – to a Californian jack-of-all-trades named George King. Tall, handsome and clever, King was only five years older than Ned; but he had already led what was to an Australian a dazzlingly rich life, as a veteran of the American Civil War, ex-circus stunt rider and expert horse-thief.

If Ned had ever really believed he could keep his nose clean, he was sunk now. His stepfather was a temptation to crime and success that he could not resist. The two men shared many values, especially their hatred for all policemen, landowners, judges and 'that old tart on her throne in England'. And within a few weeks they had exchanged all their respective secrets about the associated arts of horse-stealing – from the faking of horses' brands with needle and iodine, to the finer points of local bush-craft required to lead herds of stolen horses invisibly through the bush.

George had been doing well by himself, but with Ned riding alongside him, the operation flourished into the most successful horse-stealing ring ever seen in the colony of Victoria. It was now that Ned's 'flashness' began to find its real outlet. In one quick year, more than 280 horses were spirited away, re-branded and sold on – this in the days when a prime horse was worth the equivalent of tens of thousands of pounds in today's money.

Dismayed at this eruption of larceny, the big ranch owners now formed a league for their mutual protection, offering big cash rewards for the capture of the thieves, and petitioning the government to send more policemen out to their district.

The rich ranchmen would get no help from their poor neighbours, whose stock the horse thieves never touched. For the poor farmers were having a bad time of it themselves that year. The great drought of 1876 was burning off all the common grazing, and the big ranch owners had taken to seizing any thirsty cow or horse that strayed on to their own well-watered pastures. In the strife between rich and poor, Ned, like generations of bushrangers before him, came to be the champion of the poor settlers. He was taking the rich men on, and making them whine.

As the tension mounted, a senior police officer came all the way from Melbourne to visit the Kellys' hut, to serve a warning they were stepping up their vigilance against the family. There were one or two dust-ups in the street between Ned and various constables, but no charges arose from these scuffles, only a deepening of old resentments and a further stacking up of scores to settle.

After one fight, Constable Lonigan dragged the semi-conscious Ned across the street by his balls. The next day, when he saw Lonigan, Ned shouted after him, 'I never shot a man yet, Lonigan. But if I ever do, you'll be the first.'

# Stringybark Creek Massacre

One dusty summer's day not long afterwards, a foolhardy young policeman rode out alone to the Kelly hut. Constable Fitzpatrick intended to kill two impossible birds with one stone: to take Dan into custody and at the same time to start wooing Dan's sister Kate, whom he fancied.

His account of the afternoon's events and the Kelly version were very different. Fitzpatrick claimed he had been on the point of arresting Dan when Ned had burst in, guns blazing; he pointed to a scratch on his wrist, which he said was a bullet wound.

The Kelly version was that the policeman had arrived drunk, boasting that he was going to put Dan away, and had then pulled pretty young Kate on to his lap. Ellen had driven him off with a shovel, striking him on the arm. The Kellys insisted that, far from having taken a gun out, Ned wasn't even there; besides, he would never have started shooting in his hut with his mother and various kids running about.

Whatever really happened, Fitzpatrick's account was officially believed and Ned and Dan, on the strength of a graze on a policeman's wrist, found themselves wanted on a charge of attempted murder, with a reward of 100 pounds on their heads.

A party of policemen were sent to arrest the brothers. But, on their arrival at the hut, when they couldn't find the boys, they arrested Ellen instead – along with her Irish farmhand, and one of her daughters' husbands – and charged them with having aided and abetted the attempted murder. This was a blatant stitch-up. The authorities knew Fitzpatrick was an unreliable witness; in fact, a few months later, he was sacked for being 'a disgrace to the force'.

Ned, hiding out nearby, was so enraged at his mother's arrest that he sent word that he would turn himself in if she was released. The deal was turned down and from their hideout Ned and Dan learned how their mother had received a sentence of three years and how the judge had declared: 'If your son Ned was here, I would make an example of him. I would give him a sentence of 15 years.'

Ned knew he could never expect justice in an Australian court. If the judge was ready to put him away for so long on the word of a liar then he had no choice but to leave home and civilisation for good; in short, to become an outlaw.

\*\*\*

Riding off into the wilderness, the Kelly brothers were soon joined by two other young men. Joe Byrne and Steve Hart, both Irishmen, who had idolised Ned since boyhood. They weren't wanted for attempted murder or for any other charge; they joined the Kellys purely for the adventure. In fact it was many months before the police even knew that they were hiding out with Ned and Dan.

Each of these four young men was highly individual, and together they made one of the most compact and classic gangs of all time. Ned was indisputably the leader; the oldest by a few years, strong and charismatic. With his thick hair licked back over his head, rockabilly style, his fiery dark eyes and black spade of a beard, he looked like an early Hell's Angel on horseback.

Dan was slighter than Ned, unpredictable and a little nervy. He was very crafty, however, and loved his brother with all his tenacious heart.

Steve was tall and dark, the best rider ever known in those parts. He wore fancy clothes, and later, when there was a huge price on his head, he liked to turn up in his favourite pubs, and have a drink with his old pals as if nothing had happened, disappearing again before anyone could alert the police. Legend had it that sometimes Steve would dress up as a woman, and thus disguised he would reconnoitre for the gangs' raids.

Joe, the fourth member, was pale and quiet, always remembered as a good boy. He loved reading and writing, and it was Joe who became the brains behind the gang's exploits. He plotted their adventures, writing and re-writing the sequence of events as if they were stage-plays.

And he was the only one that Ned would go to hell for. Dan and Steve were solid characters, but Joe, the slight one, was exceptional – a fact Ned confirmed two years later, when tying a policeman up.

'Tell me, Ned,' asked the policeman before the gag was put into his mouth, 'who's your most reliable man, is it your brother?'

'No,' said Ned, and pointed at Joe Byrne. 'That bloke is as straight and true as steel.'

So these four young men headed far into the outback to make a hideout in the Wombat Ranges. They took over an abandoned gold-prospector's hut and refurbished it as a little fortress, thickening the walls with logs which would withstand bullets and armour-plating the door with a huge slab of iron. They cut slits in the walls to shoot from, and friends supplied them with all the stores they would need to endure a long siege: guns, ammunition, food and water. They practised sharp-shooting at targets pinned on the trees. They did a bit of panning in the creek and found a little gold. For several months, they lived in wonderful, undisturbed freedom.

As soon as Ned and Dan had gone into hiding, the police had mounted a desultory search of the Kelly country. Gradually they realised that the boys were being shielded by a network of sympathisers, who were feeding the gang with information about police movements and provisions. The police chiefs covered their failure by exaggerating the extent of this bush telegraph support. So, when the newspapers and politicians asked why the two Kelly ruffians were still at large after many months, the police protested that their job was very hard when half the population were helping the criminals – a slander which deepened public support for the outlaws.

Eventually the police picked up enough information to narrow their search down, and two fresh search teams were sent out into the Wombat Ranges. One party, headed by the expert tracker Sergeant Kennedy travelled up the banks of Stringybark Creek and pitched their tents in an old gold-miners' clearing, unaware that this was barely two miles from the Kelly hideout.

An air of desolation hung over the clearing,

several felled gum trees still lay on the ground, others had been ring-barked and were standing half dead. The police rolled some tree trunks into a circle around their camp fire. The plan was this: while two policemen scoured the bush, there would always be another two keeping guard back at the camp.

Days passed, and then, one afternoon, one of the two men left behind to guard the camp decided to relieve the tedium by taking pop shots at passing cockatoos. It was a blunder typical of the Victorian police efforts to track the Kelly gang down; it never occurred to him that the gunshots could alert the outlaws to his presence.

Following the sound of the shots, the Kellys crept through the bush right up to the police camp, where they saw the two guards slumped around a dying fire. With guns cocked, the Kelly gang were able to walk right in.

'Bail up!' Ned called out – the Australian for 'Stick 'em up!' The policemen lifted their hands into the air.

'Well, look who it is,' said Ned, 'Constable Lonigan.'

While Ned disarmed the two men, Steve and Dan searched the tents. In one tent Dan found a cache of weapons. Ned went to look at them.

'That's quite a few guns for a pissy little police outing,' he said, when he returned to the captives. 'Looks like you came to shoot something more than just cockatoos.'

'We didn't come to *shoot* you, we came to arrest you,' one of the policemen said, measuredly.

'And how many more of you are there in the bush?' sneered Ned. 'I promise you I'll shoot you if you don't tell me the truth.'

'Two more,' said Lonigan.

Ned sat on a log with his gun on his knee. 'Sit down,' he told his captives, at which point Dan, Steve and Joe melted into the bush to take up their posts.

'Now I won't shoot anyone who does what I say,' said Ned. 'You came to shoot me, I damn well know it, but I'm only going to take your guns and horses. Then you can go free, provided you promise to leave the police force once you get back. If you don't promise me that I'll shoot you now. And if you break your promise, I'll shoot you later. Is that settled?'

The two policemen nodded assent, but Lonigan didn't believe any of it, he felt sure that Ned intended to shoot him there and then.

When a couple of hours later they heard the noise of two men returning through the bush Lonigan did a desperate thing – before his colleagues reached the clearing, he shouted out a warning: 'Don't come any closer, Ned Kelly's here!'

Ned shot him on the spot, and Lonigan fell down dead. The two returning policemen pulled their guns and began firing from the bush. But the gang members were well positioned to shoot, and first one policeman fell, and then the other. In the dying moments of the gun-fight, the fourth policeman, who had stayed frozen by the fire, seized a horse and escaped through the scrub. A day later he reached the nearest town, from where he raised the alarm.

\*\*\*

The cold-blooded shooting of three policemen created a wave of scandal not only across Australia but around the world – Ned Kelly was now wanted not just to satisfy some petty police grudge, but on an indisputable charge of triple murder. The authorities, shamed by their failure to have caught up with the Kelly brothers earlier, demanded that the police apprehend the outlaws immediately.

Thus began the greatest man-hunt in Australian history. The greatest comedy show, too. Eighty policemen were involved full time in the hunt, and their only achievement was to keep the colony of Victoria amused.

On one occasion, 50 policemen surrounded a hut where the Kellys were believed to be. Come dawn a contingent of police stormed inside, and after a few minutes' silence a terrible gun battle began. Gingerly, more police crept up, and started firing off their guns. Several hours later shame-faced police chiefs had to admit that the hut had been empty all along, and their men had only been firing at each other.

For the next two years Ned and his gang defied capture and played the game of tag with such relish that the hunt became a sort of national pastime and spectator sport. Ned was hailed as a hero. And while he and the gang played to the gallery, taunting the police by riding along with their search parties quite undisguised, people of all sorts joined in and added to the confusion, gleefully sending the police off in the wrong direction.

Old boyhood mates from Greta turned up at newspaper offices in Melbourne to say that Ned would never be caught. Ned was tougher than ox-hide, they said, and had more cunning and bush-craft than a whole mounted regiment of colonial policemen. At 15, he had chucked a gang of them around like dung around a paddock and now he was 23 he was crafty enough, and bullish enough, to finish all the police off for good.

It is a testament of Ned's magnetism – the same quality, perhaps, which has kept his memory alive for so long – that not at any point did any of his three fellow gang members think of bailing out and handing himself in. This was Ned's great gift: whatever they were doing, no matter how perilous their lives became, he somehow managed to make everything seem like a fantastic adventure, to keep the pleasure coming. As time went on, and the reward for the gang's capture grew steadily higher, eventually reaching the colossal sum of

3,000 pounds on Ned's head, the boys realised they were all being led by slow degrees to an early death – they would not be able to escape the police for ever – but they didn't give a damn. They were having too good a time to worry about that.

# The Bushrangers

In the early days of the penal colony, the convicts had suffered two things more sharply than the hunger and the floggings – the lack of anything new to talk about, and the craving for some thing or person to satisfy their deep desire for revenge. The monotony of their existence combined with their utter powerlessness created a sort of dull existential agony from which there was no release.

To begin with, few convicts tried to break out. There was hardly any point, when all they would find beyond the prison walls was miles and miles of uncultivated scrubland. But as the colony gradually established itself and grew in prosperity, the first few convicts did begin to escape, and live in the bush. These runaways, who survived by preying off travellers, were the first bushrangers and they became the convicts' heroes – not only providing something to talk about, but acting as agents of vengeance, for they would sometimes return to the prisons and the convict-farms to kill the notoriously cruel masters.

Over time, the tales of the bushrangers were inevitably exaggerated and many crude brutes were transformed into creatures as colourful and beguiling as stage-pirates. But some bush-rangers did create genuine sensations in their lifetimes.

Matthew Brady, one of the first bush-rangers of Tasmania, responded to a government campaign to catch him by pinning up his own **WANTED** posters on which he offered a barrel of drink to anyone who brought him the body of the Governor.

Frank Gardiner, another immortal in the bush-rangers' Hall of Fame, stuck up the Government Gold Escort in 1862, a robbery so audacious that to general Australian glee it even got reported in the London *Times*.

Australia idolised its bushrangers. A newcomer could achieve instant and enduring fame for the originality of just one raid. Captain Melville became famous overnight for his bailing up of an entire sheep station with only one assistant.

Almost all the famous bushrangers ended their lives in a hail of bullets. And many songs were composed to commemorate a bush-ranger's last stand.

*The Sergeant and the Corporal they did their men divide*
*Some fired at him from behind, and some from every side*
*The Sergeant and the Corporal they both fired at him too*
*And a rifle bullet pierced the heart of bold Jack Donahoe.*

By Ned Kelly's time, this tradition of out-laws fighting an unjust system was drying up. There were the occasional bright remnants – Harry Power, for example – but generally it seemed that no one had the balls to be a bushranger any more. A newspaper story from the time gives an example of the deterioration.

A man walks into a bank and points a gun at the cashier.

'Bail up,' he says, 'and give me all your money.'

The cashier looks at the robber, smiles a little smile, then vaults the counter and chases the robber down the street, before trussing him up, gun and all, in front of a laughing crowd.

The new generation of aspiring bush-rangers, it was thought, just didn't have the mettle or style. All except for one, that is.

Ned knew the bushranging lore well, and, encouraged by the adulation of the public, made a conscious decision now to play at being the last, the most popular, the greatest bushranger of them all. He would continue the fight of his great antecedents with the easy flamboyance of a true, carefree son of the Australian soil. He would revive all the old bushranging traditions, and crown them with one new innovation of his own which would make his name and figure unforgettable.

Ned's inspiration was to dress his gang in suits of protective black armour, thick enough to see them through a lifetime of ambushes and shoot-outs. With this simple, brilliant idea, he embedded himself at a stroke in the eternal consciousness of the world.

Over many weeks, on the darkest nights, the gang and their supporters stole some 50 ploughshares from unsympathetic farmers and distributed them around a network of friendly blacksmiths. The blacksmiths then forged and beat and riveted them into breast-plates, backplates and helmets. Hours were spent at the task, the gang flitting from forge to forge to be measured and fitted.

At last, when the night-work was done, and Ned put his armour on for the first time and walked out into the sun-flooded bush, Steve, Dan and Joe reckoned that in all the history of the world there had never been anyone as unstoppable as this iron-coated bull of a man. This was the bushranger recast for the machine age, from whose face shone the slit-eyed determination of a boiler-plated knight, and inside whose breast burnt a heart as vengeful as a furnace. Mounted on his horse, Ned looked as indestructible as the steam locomotives that tilted through the Australian wilderness.

# The Bank Raids

Over the next few months, as the Kelly gang gained in confidence, their raids became increasingly daring and extraordinary. There was nearly always a Robin Hood element to their raids – Ned had intended from the start that the gang would distribute the spoils of their robberies among the poor, and they lived up to this promise. But as time went on, they also added an extra dramatic twist to their performance: each raid became an 'event' in itself, a spectacle which people would continue to talk about for years to come.

One fine morning, the four of them rode up to Younghusband's station, a set of farm buildings on a sheep-station, three miles from the little town of Euroa. Ned sauntered into the main building. There was nothing unusual about this, the farm stations of Australia had a similar feeling to the ranches in old Westerns; half-edgy, half-relaxed communities of working men where a stranger excited intense curiosity behind a veil of indifference. Besides, the gang were not yet in their armour (though they carried it with them wherever they went, in four large duffel bags slung over their horses' backs).

Ned was the first to break the silence. 'I don't suppose you know who I am.'

The farm manager scratched his head: it was a strange question. 'Perhaps you're Ned Kelly,' he replied, attempting a joke.

'That's a damn good guess,' laughed Ned, and he flashed his revolver in the sun. Now Ned sat down to eat some lunch. A few minutes later, he pushed the plate away and ambled out into the yard.

Everyone was hypnotised by his confidence. And everything remained strangely relaxed. Without hurry or anxiety, the gang rounded up the farm hands and escorted them into a slab hut. One of them stayed lookout, and if anyone approached the farm, they were invited inside the hut, to take their place on the bench along the wall.

The first night Ned stayed in the shed with his prisoners, and chatted about his adventures. No one yet knew what the purpose of this strange visit was.

The next day, leaving Joe behind, Ned, Dan and Steve chopped down the poles carrying the telegraph lines along the railway track from Euroa and then rode into town. There, they strolled into the bank, and bailed up the clerks and the manager. They also took the manager's wife hostage, along with their five children, plus a mother-in-law and three servants. They carried away 2,000 pounds in cash and 30 ounces of gold, and emptied the bank of every mortgage they could find. These were the documents which recorded how much every small farmer owed the bank as loans. By taking them Ned effectively wrote off the debts of every small farmer in the region.

The hostages and the gang then drove in a convoy of buggies back to Younghusband's station, where they lit a bonfire on which they burnt some evidence, and all the mortgages. Before they left the station, Ned asked his hostages for three hours' grace in which to make their escape, before anyone raised the alarm. They made off as night fell, at full gallop.

Never had a bank been robbed with such nonchalance. When an astonished press arrived a few days later to interview the victims of the raid, they pressed the bank manager's wife for a lurid description of her ordeal. All she would say was, 'They were perfect gentlemen.'

Australia's greatest writer of that time, Marcus Clarke, had recently written of the famous high-wayman Barrington: 'He robbed with grace and broke the eighth commandment with an air.' But no one had ever rivalled the grace of Ned Kelly, or robbed a bank with such good manners or good humour.

The police, still without any lead to follow, resorted to imprisoning friends and relatives of the gang, simply on suspicion of their having helped the outlaws. As an attempt to starve the gang out of the bush this was not only ineffectual – by now there were far too many Kelly sympathisers out there to contend with – it made the police even more unpopular.

It also served to feed Ned Kelly's anger. Nowadays, when it came to the police, and the Australian authorities, Ned was not just abusive and cynical. He was beginning to show a whole new side of his character: full of anger and bile. At one point, he addressed a long, bitter letter to the nation's politicians, which charged:

'You are committing a manifest injustice in imprisoning so many innocent people just because they are supposed to be friendly to us... I warn you that within a week we will leave your colony, but we will not leave it until we have made the country ring with the name of Kelly and taken terrible revenge for the injustice and oppression we have been subjected to. Beware, for we are now desperate men.'

\*\*\*

But Ned wouldn't carry out this threat, yet. His next move, seven weeks later, was to rob another bank, this time in the neighbouring colony of New South Wales, so as to humiliate the police force there, too. The Jerilderie bank robbery was even more brazen and coolly planned than the raid at Euroa. Ned Kelly made bank stick-ups into street-parties.

The gang rode into Jerilderie, a small, dusty town, one fine February evening. First they stopped off at the pub, and, while chatting with the regulars, learned the names of the town's two policemen. At closing time they rode up to the police station and shouted out: 'Mr Devine, there's a row on at Davidson's Hotel. Come quick, or there'll be murder!'

The two policemen had been asleep, and as they tumbled out of the station, the outlaws bailed them up at gunpoint. They were hand-cuffed and led into the cells, and the gang installed themselves in the station.

The next day was a Sunday. Having borrowed the policemen's uniforms, the gang walked about the town pretending to be special constables just arrived in the district. Monday morning was much the same; they wandered around, stopping by the black-smith to get their horses re-shod, buying bits and pieces from various shops and charging them to the police account.

At noon on Monday, the party entered the Royal

Mail Hotel, and informed the landlord that they would be sticking up the bank in the afternoon, and would require his premises as a temporary jail in which to hold the towns-people during the raid. Dan posted himself out in the street, and each time a passer-by came abreast, he showed them his gun, and gestured them into the hotel bar, where Steve stood guard over the growing crowd. The barman was told to give everyone drinks, on the Kellys.

Ned and Joe then strolled round to the bank next door, bailed up the cashiers and proceeded to empty the bank of all its cash. During the raid, a customer walked in.

'Who are you?' Ned asked.

'My name's Elliott, I'm the schoolmaster. I've come to withdraw some money.'

Ned smiled, 'You're too late, Ned Kelly has just withdrawn it all!'

Next Ned found a drawer, which seemed to be full of mortgages. He bundled them up, declaring they would make a fine bonfire. One of the bank clerks let out a little cry at this, and begged Ned not to burn them.

'Why not?' Ned asked.

The bank manager piped up, explaining that there was no point burning the documents as the head branch now kept copies of all its mortgages. He went on and on about how few of the small farmers of New South Wales would thank him for destroying them until Ned began to feel agitated and suspicious: these dumb clerks were trying to get the better of him.

'Shut your bloody mouth!' he said, and kicked the bundle across the floor. At which point, another two men suddenly walked up to the bank. Before Dan could intercept them, the men saw what was happening and turned on their heels and fled. One of them ran straight into the hotel, and captivity, but the other vanished up the street.

Ned now ran back in alarm to the hotel and threatened to start shooting if someone didn't tell him quick who the vanished man was. It turned out he was named Gill. Joe went to check the post office to make sure Gill hadn't telegraphed anyone about the raid; and smashed the telegraph equipment while he was there. In fact, Gill was so terrified that he had run straight into the bush where he stayed hiding for a day and a night in a wombat hole.

After emptying the bank the gang retired to the hotel, where there were more drinks, and even a few speeches. Ned told the story of how he had shot Lonigan and the others at Stringybark Creek. Many in the drunken crowd cheered him when he boasted that he was shortly going to shoot the two town policemen. But, as at Euroa, they shot no one, and closed the raid simply by riding off on four heavily laden horses.

Ned did, however, leave one thing behind him at Jerilderie – a long letter justifying his life and actions. The 'Jerilderie Letter', which is about three quarters as long as this book, goes through all the significant events of his criminal life: from the parcel of calves' balls through the fight with Constable Hall and his version of how Fitzpatrick's wrist got scratched in the scuffle at his mother's hut. He even gives his version of the killing at Stringybark Creek and expresses the hope that if the authorities knew the story from his side, they might forgive him.

But even Ned knew that this would never happen. When he had shot those three policemen, he had crossed a line over which there would be no return. And yet… and yet… if only the police could have behaved decently and honestly in the first place.

Despite his pleas for mercy, Ned frequently loses his temper in the letter, calling the police 'big, ugly, fat-necked, wombat-headed, big-bellied, magpie-legged, narrow-hipped, splay-footed sons of Irish bailiffs or English landlords'.

In one passage, where his indignant blood has risen very high, he delivers a terrible warning: 'In every paper that is printed I am called the blackest and coldest-blooded murderer ever on record. But if I hear any more of it I will not exactly show them what cold-blooded murder is… but wholesale and retail slaughter… something different to shooting three troopers in self-defence and robbing a bank.'

The bank raids at Euroa and Jerilderie had been such masterpieces of organisation, and so popular, that Ned now planned to give the people of Australia something they would talk about forever.

Ned had always known that he and the gang could not escape capture indefinitely. A shoot-out with the police at some point was inevitable. In which case, he thought, he would stage the encounter at his own convenience. He would have the gang reveal themselves in their black armour at a place and a time of their own choosing; and, as the police flocked to catch them, so the general slaughter would begin.

# Glenrowan Bail-up

By now several Aboriginal black-trackers from Queensland had joined the hunt for the Kelly gang. These wily bush-men could follow a man's trail even though it was several days old, and Ned knew to respect their skill. The police were definitely edging closer – not least because they had managed to put together their own network of spies and helpers, among them one particular young man who had been feeding them invaluable information.

Aaron Sherrit was Joe Byrne's oldest friend, and, in the early months of the hunt for the Kelly brothers, he had worked as a double agent for the gang, seeming to help the police but only so as to pass on to Ned information about police movements. Now, though, the gang suspected that he had switched sides, and gone over to the police.

In order to find out one way or the other, Joe Byrne rode up to Aaron's mother's house on the road outside Beechworth, and warned her, 'I'm going to kill Aaron.' Immediately, Aaron was given an around-the-clock police guard. As far as the gang was concerned, this was confirmation of his treachery.

Ned and Joe now drew up an elaborate plan to use the murder of Aaron as the bait to draw large numbers of police after them. The details were worked out with blood-chilling precision. Again and again Joe wrote and rewrote the plan, until it appeared infallible.

So one Saturday night, Joe and Dan rode into Beechworth and took hostage a hapless German friend of Aaron's. They dragged him to Aaron's house and knocked on the door.

'Who is it?' Aaron asked from inside.

'Only me,' said the hostage, a gun sticking in his belly.

When Aaron opened the door, Joe shot him twice. The four policemen guarding Aaron were no protection at all: at the first shot, they all scrambled under Aaron's bed, where they remained hiding until morning.

Meanwhile, Ned and Steve had gone on in advance to Glenrowan – a small railroad halt situated about 12 miles before Beechworth on the Melbourne-Beechworth line – which was to be the site of the next raid. They had bailed up the station-master, rounded up a few rail-road labourers, and set them to work removing a section of line on a curve in the track just outside the town. The position of the sabotage to the railway line, right above a gorge on the Beechworth side of the town, was carefully planned. Ned figured that as soon as the police chiefs heard of Aaron's murder they would cram a special train full of constables and black-trackers, and steam at high speed towards the town of Beechworth to catch the trail before it went cold.

Charging through Glenrowan at about 50 miles an hour, the train would then spill off the broken tracks, and down the ravine, killing everyone inside it – all the big, ugly, fat-necked, wombat-headed, big-bellied, magpie-legged, narrow-hipped, splay-footed sons of Irish bailiffs or English landlords, better known as officers of the Victoria police. Ned would be listening for the sound of the train passing through, and then for the crash, as he held the townspeople prisoner in one of the Glenrowan hotels, and feasted them with booze.

\*\*\*

Everything was to happen just as Ned anticipated – the special train did set off from Melbourne for Beechworth, full of policemen and black-trackers. But it was not within the timescale he had expected. For Ned, despite his long familiarity with their form, had not been prepared for the endemic cowardice and inefficiency of the Victoria Police. If the four men guarding Aaron had raised the alarm sooner, then many police lives would indeed have been taken.

After spending the Saturday night trembling under Aaron's bed, one of the four policemen eventually plucked up the courage to ride into

Beechworth and report the murder. He got to the telegraph office just before Sunday lunchtime, so that when the wires reached the senior officers in Melbourne, one and all were snoozing off a large lunch. Once these oafs were roused, such chaos ensued that it was not until ten o'clock on Sunday evening, a good 24 hours after Aaron's murder, that the train actually set out on its long journey to Beechworth, stopping to collect various contingents of police and trackers, journalists and horses along the way. There were many other delays and typical police blunders – men and horses charging into one another in the dark, carriages uncoupled from locomotives, trains switched to the wrong track – all of which, unbeknownst to the police, saved their lives.

After bailing up the entire town of Glenrowan, Ned and Steve waited for Joe and Dan to join them, hotfoot from their shooting of Aaron. The gang then kept everyone waiting throughout Sunday for the special train to come. In the afternoon there were running and jumping games outside, and in the evening the dancing began. A carnival spirit was forced on to the occasion; the atmosphere was alternately tense and calm. None of the hostages knew what was going to happen. The round-up of townspeople in the bar had seemed to follow the pattern of the gang's earlier raids in Euroa and Jerilderie. But there was no bank in Glenrowan; the town had nothing but a couple of pubs and a railway stop – what had the Kelly gang come for?

The gang themselves appeared relaxed. Perhaps deep down they were relieved that the two years of hiding and running were over, that the first stage of their showdown with the police was about to begin. As they drank the hours away, friendships formed between hostages and the gang members. One or two hostages asked if they could nip home for a while, to do some chore or other; to water the horse, or feed grandma. Ned waved them out with a friendly smile, barely making them promise to return. It seemed that as long as you weren't a policeman, Ned would trust you.

But the waiting continued; it seemed to go on forever, and as Sunday night wore away the gang grew increasingly alarmed about the non-appearance of the train. They began to exchange nervous looks, to talk in hushed tones between themselves about whether they hadn't better be going. Maybe they had miscalculated the police reaction to the shooting of Aaron Sherrit, and the police were planning to stalk up on them from another direction?

Inside the pub the pretence that everyone was enjoying themselves became more and more forced, as the people sensed something was going wrong. A few tried to cheer the atmosphere by singing old bushranging songs. One old gold prospector, very drunk, called out, 'Come on, who'll join me in a chorus of Bold Jack Donahoe?'

Ned smiled, but his lips were too dry to sing, and the song fizzled out. Then another man approached Ned.

'My wife's ill,' he said. 'If you don't mind I should get back to her.'

Ned, unimpressed by the man's broad smile, looked around the party. 'Has this man got a sick wife?' he asked them. One or two heads nodded tentatively.

'I'll be straight back, I promise,' said the man. 'I'm with you, Ned, heart and soul.'

Ned looked him up and down. What was his name?

'Thomas. Thomas Curnow.'

'All right,' Ned said at last. 'You go. But make sure you come straight back.'

Over the next few hours, the forced jollity in the bar subsided almost completely as people realised the gang had one interest alone, which was to listen for a noise from outside. All four of the gang became utterly distracted, their ears straining to catch the sound of the train bowling through the town to perdition.

It never came; in the small hours of Monday morning a wholly unexpected noise startled the anxious hush. It was the long, shrill whistle of a locomotive coming to a halt. The train was standing right outside the pub.

'That bastard Curnow's given us away,' said Dan.

Without a pause the gang disappeared into a back room. The hushed audience heard a strange ominous clanking, and a few minutes later the four men re-emerged, dressed in their black, iron over-coats – four horsemen of the imminent apocalypse.

# Capture

Thomas Curnow's name is still a pretty dirty one in some places in Australia, for, by saving that train, he pretty well made certain the police would catch Ned Kelly. He had worked out what was going on from the gang's conversations, and once out of the hotel he had tied his sister's red scarf around a lantern, and walked up the railway line waving it in the dark. The driver saw his beacon, and managed to stop the train.

As soon as they reached the pub, the police opened up their guns directly into it, even though they knew that at least 40 hostages were being held inside. The possibility that they had finally got the

Kelly gang in their sights was the sweetest feeling: they weren't going to let a group of innocent hostages stand in their way.

The bullets went straight through the walls. As soon as the first shot was fired, the lights were put out in the pub, and there followed a nightmarish scene as the iron-clad outlaws stalked through the dark rooms, impervious to the gunfire, while one by one their hostages were hit.

Occasionally one or two hostages, unable to bear the carnage any longer, dashed out of the pub, waving their arms and shouting that there were unarmed townspeople inside; the police did not seem to hear or care, and sporadic firing continued.

One of the policemen was heard shouting out in glee, 'I've shot Mother Jones in the tits!'

After several hours the firing slowed down, but no movement came from either side. Joe Byrne, despite his armour, had been hit in the groin and he died at the bar, the first of the gang to fall. Ned had left the pub at this time, and was working his way behind police lines. Alone, through the mist and smoke of that Monday dawn, he appeared from behind the police marksmen, and slowly walked towards them.

At first no one could be sure who, or what, he was; some thought he was the devil coming out of the half-light, some thought he was a crazy black man. If nothing else, the apparition had the effect of diverting the dazed policemen. At the sight of that bucket-headed black stump approaching at such a deliberate, funereal pace, all 30 officers stopped pouring lead into the pub walls and turned their guns towards its grim, mysterious outline instead.

As their bullets hit their mark, a dull noise rang through the air like a mud-caked bell. Still the shape came towards them, waving a gun in the air, but not firing. His behaviour was like that of a hunted bear who, having lost the strength to run further, has one thing only on his mind, to turn on his hunters, to pursue them, and, when he has his arms wrapped around them all, to throw himself over the precipice.

Still Ned came, while nine policemen stood around him firing in a ring. Then, one of them began to shoot at his legs, which were not protected. And he fell. It was only when they pulled his helmet off that they knew for sure they'd got Ned Kelly.

Not long afterwards Steve and Dan were shot through the walls of the pub. And at last the gunfire stopped. No one dared go in. The ruined building, a rick of splinters, was set alight. The burnt corpses of the three out-laws were dragged out later that day. The police mounted a guard over their burnt remains, but a large crowd came to claim them and the police did not dare stop them.

Anyway, they had the man they wanted – alive. Back at the station Ned Kelly was examined; he was wounded in the arm, hand and legs, and his body was covered in bruises from all the hits his armour had taken. He was bloody, and sooty, and very weak. They undressed him, and washed him down.

'What's this, Ned?' asked one of the policemen, fingering a bloody ribbon of green material he had found among Ned's clothes.

When Ned showed no sign of answering, the same policeman turned to his colleague, 'What do you make of it?'

'Don't know,' his pal replied. 'Must have been a sash once. Green and gold. Some holy Mick rag.'

***

A few months later, Ned was tried on a single charge – for the murder of Constable Lonigan – to which he pleaded not guilty. The trial was expected to last one day. In fact it took two. The result was inevitable.

In a newspaper article printed a few weeks before he was hung, Ned reflected on the moral to be drawn from his short life. For once, he kept his anger at bay. Coolly and dispassionately, he wrote: 'If my life teaches the public that men are made mad by bad treatment, and if the police are taught that they may exasperate to madness men they prosecute and ill-treat, my life will not be entirely thrown away.'

# Key Dates

1780  First Prison ships arrive in Australia

1841  Red Kelly deported from Ireland

1851  Australian Gold Rush

1854  Birth of Ned

1865  Ned pulls Dick Shelton from the creek

1866  Death of Red

1867  Ned sent to Beechworth jail

1876  Ned teams up with his American stepfather

1878  Stringybark Creek massacre

From 1994 to 2000, Charlie Boxer wrote
and published a series of history magazines for
teenagers called Orange Blossom Special, on
subjects ranging from the courtiers of medieval
Japan to American railroad bums. His first novel,
*The Cloud of Dust*, was published in 2002
by Jonathan Cape, and is now available
in Vintage paperback.

Dear Reader,

No matter how old you are, good books always leave you wanting to know more. If you have any questions you would like to ask the author, **Charlie Boxer,** about **Ned Kelly** please write to us at: SHORT BOOKS 15 Highbury Terrace, London N5 1UP.

If you enjoyed this title, then you would probably enjoy others in the series. Why not click on our website for more information and see what the teachers are being told? **www.theshortbookco.com**

All the books in the WHO WAS... series are available from TBS, Distribution Centre, Colchester Road, Frating Green, Colchester, Essex CO7 7DW (Tel: 01206 255800), at £4.99 + P&P.

OTHER TITLES IN THE **WHO WAS...** SERIES:

**WHO WAS... Admiral Nelson**
**The Sailor Who Dared All to Win**
**Sam Llewellyn**
1-904095-65-8

No one ever imagined that a weak skinny boy like
Horatio Nelson would be able to survive the hardships
of life at sea. But he did. In fact he grew up to become
a great naval hero, the man who saved Britain from
invasion by the dreaded Napoleon.

Nelson was someone who always did things his own
way. He lost an eye and an arm in battle, but never let
that hold him back. He was brilliant on ships, clumsy
on land, ferocious in battle, knew fear but overcame it,
and never, never took no for an answer.

This is his story.

**WHO WAS... David Livingstone**
**The Legendary Explorer**
**Amanda Mitchison**
**1-904095-84-4**

Born a poor Glasgow cotton-mill worker, David grew up to become a great explorer and hero of his time.

This is his incredible story. The tough man of Victorian Britain would stop at nothing in his determination to be the first white man to explore Afirca, even if it meant dragging his wife and children along with him.

He trekked hundreds of miles through dangerous territory, braving terrible illness and pain, and was attacked by cannibals, rampaging lions and killer ants...

**WHO WAS... Anne Boleyn**
**The Queen Who Lost her Head**
**Laura Beatty**
**1-904095-78-X**

For Anne Boleyn, King Henry VIII threw away his wife, out-
raged his people, chucked his religion, and drove his best
friend to death.

What does it take to drive a King this crazy?
Was she a witch? An enchantress? Whatever she was,
Anne turned Tudor England upside-down and shook it.
And everyone was talking about her...

But Anne lived dangerously. And when she could
not give the King the one thing he wanted – a son –
his love went out like a light. The consequences for
Anne were deadly...

**WHO WAS... Alexander Selkirk**
**Survivor on a Desert Island**
**Amanda Mitchison**
**1-904095-79-8**

On the beach stood a wild thing waving its arms and hollering. The thing had the shape of a man, but it was all covered in fur, like a Barbary ape. What was it? A new kind of animal? A monster?

It was Alexander Selkirk, Scottish mariner and adventurer, thrilled to be rescued by passing sailors after four years alone on a Pacific island. This is the story of how Selkirk came to be stranded on the island and how he survived, the story of...
THE REAL ROBINSON CRUSOE.

**WHO WAS... Ada Lovelace**
**Computer Wizard of Victorian England**
**Lucy Lethbridge**
1-904095-76-3

Daughter of the famous poet Lord Byron, Ada
Lovelace was a child prodigy. Brilliant at maths, she
read numbers like most people read words.

In 1834 she came to the attention of Charles Babbage,
a scientist and techno0whizz who had just built an
amazing new 'THINKING MACHINE'. Ada and Mr
Babbage made a perfect partnership, which produced
the most important invention of the modern world –
THE COMPUTER!

*WINNER OF THE BLUE PETER*
*BOOK AWARD 2002!*

**WHO WAS... Charlotte Brontë**
**The Girl Who Turned her Life into a Book**
**Kate Hubbard**
**1-904095-80-1**

Of the famous Bronte siblings, Charlotte, the eldest, was the survivor. At eight, she was packed off to a boarding school so harsh that it killed two of her sisters. Her adult years were equally haunted by tragedy.

But one thing kept Charlotte going: she had a secret talent for story-telling. This is the tale of a remarkable woman, who turned her own life into one of the world's greatest classic novels, *Jane Eyre*.

## OTHER TITLES IN THE WHO WAS... SERIES

Emily Davison
The girl who gave her life for her cause
Claudia FitzHerbert
1-904095-66-6

Sam Johnson
The wonderful word doctor
Andrew Billen
1-904095-77-1

Annie Oakley
Sharpshooter of the Wild West
Lucy Lethbridge
1-904095-60-7

William Shakespeare
The mystery of the world's greatest playwright
Rupert Christiansen
1-904095-81-X

Queen Victoria
The woman who ruled the world
Kate Hubbard
1-904095-82-2

Florence Nightingale
The lady with the lamp
Charlotte Moore
1-904095-83-6

Madame Tussaud
Waxwork queen of the French Revolution
Tony Thorne
1-904095-85-2

Nelson Mandela
The prisoner who became a president
Adrian Hadland
1-904095-86-0

The Bloody Baron
Evil invader of the East
Nick Middleton
1-904095-87-9